MW00466311

DAYBREAK
VERSES

for MEN

Titles in this series:

DAYBREAK
VERSES

for MEN

Compiled by LARRY RICHARDS

ZONDERVAN®

ZONDERVAN

DayBreak Verses for Men
Copyright © 2012 by Zondervan
All rights reserved

This title is also available as a Zondervan ebook.
Visit www.zondervan.com/ebooks.

Requests for information should be addressed to:

Zondervan, *Grand Rapids, Michigan* 49530

Library of Congress Catalog Card Number 2012939818

Any Internet addresses (websites, blogs, etc.) and telephone numbers in this
book are offered as a resource. They are not intended in any way to be or
imply an endorsement by Zondervan, nor does Zondervan vouch for the
content of these sites and numbers for the life of this book.

Cover design: Jamie DeBruyn
Cover photography or illustration: istockphoto
Interior design: Nancy Wilson

Printed in the United States of America

12 13 14 15 16 17 18 /DPM/ 12 11 10 9 8 7 6 5 4 3 2 1

You are a special person.
You are loved by God
and have a significant place in his plan.
This booklet will help you
sense the wonder of your
identity as God's person,
and it will show you how to find
fulfillment with your spouse,
your family, your church, the world
and in your inner life.

CONTENTS

PART ONE
MY IDENTITY AS A CHRISTIAN MAN

PART TWO
MY RELATIONSHIPS AS A CHRISTIAN MAN

RELATIONSHIP WITH MY SPOUSE

PART THREE
MY INNER LIFE AS A
CHRISTIAN MAN

INTRODUCTION

What does it mean to be a Christian man? First, it means to learn to see yourself as God sees you — as a person who is loved and significant. Second, it means to understand the wonderful place God has for you in his plan. That place is found as you live out your most significant relationships guided by God's Word and strengthened by his promises. And it means to build your own inner life, developing your potentials as a Christian.

There are three sections to this booklet. In each a series of topics brings together verses from God's Word that will give you guidance, insight and strength to help you be all God intends you to be as his person.

The first section, "My Identity as a Christian Man," shares evidence that you truly are important to God and have a significant place in his kingdom.

"My Relationships as a Christian Man" looks closely at your relationship with your spouse, your family, your church and in the world. Verses from Scripture portray God's ideal and share insights on how you can live as Christ's person to achieve the ideal.

"My Inner Life as a Christian Man" focuses on deepening your personal relationship with God and on finding help from him to meet special, very personal challenges. Issues such as getting the most from Scripture, living the single life and overcoming temptations are examined.

As you read these verses and meditate on them you will find them to be a source of guidance, for God points us in his Word to a productive and meaningful life. You will also find them to be a source of strength, for here too are God's promises, reassuring you that the Lord is committed to helping you become the Christian man you yearn to be.

PART ONE

MY IDENTITY AS A CHRISTIAN MAN

When you became a Christian you began a personal relationship with God. In this wonderful relationship you can discover your true identity and your true significance. God wants you to base your confidence that you truly do have worth and value on his affirmation that you are vitally important . . . to him!

CREATED IN GOD'S IMAGE

GENESIS 1:27–28

So God created mankind in his own image, in the image of God he created them; male and female he created them. God blessed them and said to them, "Be fruitful and increase in number; fill the earth and subdue it. Rule . . ."

PSALM 8:4,6

What is mankind that you are mindful of them, human beings that you care for them? . . . You made them rulers over the works of your hands; you put everything under their feet.

PSALM 100:3

Know that the LORD is God. It is he who made us, and we are his; we are his people, the sheep of his pasture.

PSALM 119:73–74

Your hands made me and formed me; give me understanding to learn your commands. May those who fear you rejoice when they see me, for I have put my hope in your word.

PSALM 139:13–16

For you created my inmost being; you knit me together in my mother's womb. I praise you because I am fearfully and wonderfully made; your works are wonderful, I know that full well. My frame was not hidden from you when I was made in the secret place, when I was woven together in the depths of the earth. Your eyes saw my unformed body; all the days ordained for me were written in your book before one of them came to be.

LEVITICUS 19:2

"Speak to the entire assembly of Israel and say to them: 'Be holy because I, the LORD your God, am holy.'"

_____SAVED BY CHRIST'S SACRIFICE_____

EPHESIANS 2:4–5

But because of his great love for us, God, who is rich in mercy, made us alive with Christ even when we were dead in transgressions — it is by grace you have been saved.

GALATIANS 2:20

"I have been crucified with Christ and I no longer live, but Christ lives in me. The life I now live in the body, I live by faith in the Son of God, who loved me and gave himself for me."

ROMANS 8:32

He who did not spare his own Son, but gave him up for us all — how will he not also, along with him, graciously give us all things?

JOHN 3:16

For God so loved the world that he gave his one and only Son, that whoever believes in him shall not perish but have eternal life.

COLOSSIANS 1:22

But now he has reconciled you by Christ's physical body through death to present you holy in his sight, without blemish and free from accusation.

ROMANS 8:35,37–39

Who shall separate us from the love of Christ? Shall trouble or hardship or persecution or famine or nakedness or danger or sword? . . . No, in all these things we are more than conquerors through him who loved us. For I am convinced that neither death nor life, neither angels nor demons . . . nor anything else in all creation, will be able to separate us from the love of God that is in Christ Jesus our Lord.

PART OF GOD'S FAMILY

ROMANS 8:16–17

The Spirit himself testifies with our spirit that we are God's children. Now if we are children, then we are heirs — heirs of God and co-heirs with Christ, if indeed we share in his sufferings in order that we may also share in his glory.

ISAIAH 49:15

"Can a mother forget the baby at her breast and have no compassion on the child she has borne? Though she may forget, I will not forget you!"

GALATIANS 3:26–28

So in Christ Jesus you are all children of God through faith, for all of you who were baptized into Christ have clothed yourselves with Christ. There is neither Jew nor Gentile, neither slave nor free, nor is there male and female, for you are all one in Christ Jesus.

EPHESIANS 5:1–2

Follow God's example, therefore, as dearly loved children and walk in the way of love, just as Christ loved us and gave himself up for us as a fragrant offering and sacrifice to God.

1 PETER 1:14–16

As obedient children, do not conform to the evil desires you had when you lived in ignorance. But just as he who called you is holy, so be holy in all you do; for it is written: "Be holy, because I am holy."

1 JOHN 3:9

No one who is born of God will continue to sin, because God's seed remains in them; they cannot go on sinning, because they have been born of God.

_____INDWELT BY GOD'S SPIRIT_____

EZEKIEL 36:26–27

"I will give you a new heart and put a new spirit in you; I will remove from you your heart of stone and give you a heart of flesh. And I will put my Spirit in you and move you to follow my decrees and be careful to keep my laws."

JOHN 14:16–17

"The Father . . . will give you another advocate to help you and be with you forever — the Spirit of truth. The world cannot accept him, because it neither sees him nor knows him. But you know him, for he lives with you and will be in you."

ROMANS 8:26

In the same way, the Spirit helps us in our weakness. We do not know what we ought to pray for, but the Spirit himself intercedes for us through wordless groans.

ROMANS 8:11

And if the Spirit of him who raised Jesus from the dead is living in you, he who raised Christ from the dead will also give life to your mortal bodies because of his Spirit who lives in you.

GALATIANS 5:16

So I say, walk by the Spirit, and you will not gratify the desires of the flesh.

ROMANS 15:13

May the God of hope fill you with all joy and peace as you trust in him, so that you may overflow with hope by the power of the Holy Spirit.

1 CORINTHIANS 2:12

What we have received is not the spirit of the world, but the Spirit who is from God, so that we may understand what God has freely given us.

GIFTED TO SERVE OTHERS

1 CORINTHIANS 12:4–7

There are different kinds of gifts, but the same Spirit distributes them. There are different kinds of service, but the same Lord. There are different kinds of working, but in all of them and in everyone it is the same God at work. Now to each one the manifestation of the Spirit is given for the common good.

ROMANS 12:4–6

For just as each of us has one body with many members, and these members do not all have the same function, so in Christ we, though many, form one body, and each member belongs to all the others. We have different gifts, according to the grace given to each of us. If your gift is prophesying, then prophesy in accordance with your faith.

1 PETER 4:10–11

Each of you should use whatever gift you have received to serve others, as faithful stewards of God's grace in its various forms. If anyone speaks, they should do so as one who speaks the very words of God. If anyone serves, they should do so with the strength God provides, so that in all things God may be praised through Jesus Christ. To him be the glory and the power for ever and ever. Amen.

ACTS 2:17–18

"In the last days, God says, I will pour out my Spirit on all people. Your sons and daughters will prophesy, your young men will see visions, your old men will dream dreams. Even on my servants, both men and women, I will pour out my Spirit in those days, and they will prophesy."

_____CALLED TO BE A DISCIPLE_____

MATTHEW 16:24–25

Then Jesus said to his disciples, "Whoever wants to be my disciple must deny themselves and take up their cross and follow me. For whoever wants to save their life will lose it, but whoever loses their life for me will find it."

John 8:31–32

To the Jews who had believed him, Jesus said, "If you hold to my teaching, you are really my disciples. Then you will know the truth, and the truth will set you free."

Luke 6:20–22

Looking at his disciples, he said: "Blessed are you who are poor, for yours is the kingdom of God. Blessed are you who hunger now, for you will be satisfied. Blessed are you who weep now, for you will laugh. Blessed are you when people hate you, when they exclude you and insult you and reject your name as evil, because of the Son of Man."

Zephaniah 3:17

The Lord your God is with you, the Mighty Warrior who saves. He will take great delight in you; in his love he will no longer rebuke you, but will rejoice over you with singing."

John 15:5,7–8

"I am the vine; you are the branches. If you remain in me and I in you, you will bear much fruit . . . If you remain in me and my words remain in you, ask whatever you wish, and it will be done for you. This is to my Father's glory, that you bear much fruit, showing yourselves to be my disciples."

_____GUIDED THROUGH LIFE_____

PROVERBS 3:5–6

Trust in the LORD with all your heart and lean not on your own understanding; in all your ways submit to him, and he will make your paths straight.

EXODUS 15:13

"In your unfailing love you will lead the people you have redeemed. In your strength you will guide them to your holy dwelling."

PSALM 143:10

Teach me to do your will, for you are my God; may your good Spirit lead me on level ground.

PSALM 86:11–12

Teach me your way, LORD, that I may rely on your faithfulness; give me an undivided heart, that I may fear your name. I will praise you, Lord my God, with all my heart; I will glorify your name forever.

PSALM 37:4

Take delight in the LORD, and he will give you the desires of your heart.

PSALM 1:6

For the LORD watches over the way of the righteous, but the way of the wicked leads to destruction.

PSALM 25:9

He guides the humble in what is right and teaches them his way.

PSALM 25:12

Who, then, are those who fear the LORD? He will instruct them in the ways they should choose.

ISAIAH 42:16

"I will lead the blind by ways they have not known . . . I will guide them."

GUARDED BY GOD'S POWER

1 PETER 1:3–5

Praise be to the God and Father of our Lord Jesus Christ! In his great mercy he has given us new birth into a living hope through the resurrection of Jesus Christ from the dead, and into an inheritance that can never perish, spoil or fade. This inheritance is kept in heaven for you, who through faith are shielded by God's power until the coming of the salvation that is ready to be revealed in the last time.

ISAIAH 46:4

"Even to your old age and gray hairs I am he, I am he who will sustain you. I have made you and I will carry you; I will sustain you and I will rescue you."

JUDE 24

[He] is able to keep you from stumbling and to present you before his glorious presence without fault and with great joy.

DEUTERONOMY 31:6

"Be strong and courageous. Do not be afraid or terrified because of them, for the LORD your God goes with you; he will never leave you nor forsake you."

PSALM 91:1–2

Whoever dwells in the shelter of the Most High will rest in the shadow of the Almighty. I will say of the LORD, "He is my refuge and my fortress, my God, in whom I trust."

PSALM 86:2

Guard my life, for I am faithful to you; save your servant who trusts in you. You are my God.

_____GROWING MORE CHRISTLIKE_____

ROMANS 8:29

For those God foreknew he also predestined to be conformed to the image of his Son, that he might be the firstborn among many brothers and sisters.

COLOSSIANS 3:5,9–10

Put to death, therefore, whatever belongs to your earthly nature . . . You have taken off your old self with its practices and have put on the new self, which is being renewed in knowledge in the image of its Creator.

1 JOHN 3:2–3

Dear friends, now we are children of God, and what we will be has not yet been made known. But we know that when Christ appears, we shall be like him, for we shall see him as he is. All who have this hope in him purify themselves, just as he is pure.

2 CORINTHIANS 3:18

We . . . are being transformed into his image with ever-increasing glory, which comes from the Lord, who is the Spirit.

2 CORINTHIANS 3:3

You show that you are a letter from Christ, the result of our ministry, written not with ink but with the Spirit of the living God, not on tablets of stone but on tablets of human hearts.

1 PETER 4:1–2

Therefore, since Christ suffered in his body, arm yourselves also with the same attitude, because whoever suffers in the body is done with sin. As a result, they do not live the rest of their earthly lives for evil human desires, but rather for the will of God.

DESTINED FOR ETERNAL GLORY

ISAIAH 26:19

But your dead will live, LORD; their bodies will rise — let those who dwell in the dust wake up and shout for joy — your dew is like the dew of the morning; the earth will give birth to her dead.

1 CORINTHIANS 15:42–44

So will it be with the resurrection of the dead. The body that is sown is perishable, it is raised imperishable; it is sown in dishonor, it is raised in glory; it is sown in weakness, it is raised in power; it is sown a natural body, it is raised a spiritual body. If there is a natural body, there is also a spiritual body.

1 CORINTHIANS 15:54

When the perishable has been clothed with the imperishable, and the mortal with immortality, then the saying that is written will come true: "Death has been swallowed up in victory."

JEREMIAH 17:10

"I the LORD search the heart and examine the mind, to reward each person according to their conduct, according to what their deeds deserve."

2 CORINTHIANS 5:9–10

We make it our goal to please him . . . For we must all appear before the judgment seat of Christ, so that each of us may receive what is due us for the things done while in the body, whether good or bad.

2 THESSALONIANS 1:7,10

The Lord Jesus [will be] revealed from heaven in blazing fire with his powerful angels . . . He comes to be glorified in his holy people and to be marveled at among all those who have believed. This includes you, because you believed our testimony to you.

COLOSSIANS 3:4

When Christ, who is your life, appears, then you also will appear with him in glory.

PART TWO

MY RELATIONSHIPS AS A CHRISTIAN MAN

God has a shining ideal for the life of a Christian man. At times the ideal seems beyond us. But God has provided his Word to guide and his promises to strengthen. Verses focusing on relationships with spouse, family, church and world help you grow toward all God wants you to be.

RELATIONSHIP WITH MY SPOUSE

_____GOD'S IDEAL FOR MY MARRIAGE_____

GENESIS 2:18,22–24

The LORD God said, "It is not good for the man to be alone. I will make a helper suitable for him" . . . The LORD God made a woman from the rib he had taken out of the man, and he brought her to the man. The man said, "This is now bone of my bones and flesh of my flesh; she shall be called 'woman,' for she was taken out of man." That is why a man leaves his father and mother and is united to his wife, and they become one flesh.

GENESIS 24:67

Isaac brought her into the tent of his mother Sarah, and he married Rebekah. So she became his wife, and he loved her; and Isaac was comforted after his mother's death.

1 CORINTHIANS 11:11–12

Nevertheless, in the Lord woman is not independent of man, nor is man independent of woman. For as woman came from man, so also man is born of woman. But everything comes from God.

COLOSSIANS 3:12–14

Therefore, as God's chosen people, holy and dearly loved, clothe yourselves with compassion, kindness, humility, gentleness and patience. Bear with each other and forgive another if any of you has a grievance against someone. Forgive as the Lord forgave you. And over all these virtues put on love, which binds them all together in perfect unity.

MY ROLE AS A HUSBAND

1 PETER 3:7

Husbands, in the same way be considerate as you live with your wives, and treat them with respect as the weaker partner and as heirs with you of the gracious gift of life, so that nothing will hinder your prayers.

EPHESIANS 5:21

Submit to one another out of reverence for Christ.

EPHESIANS 5:25–29,33

Husbands, love your wives, just as Christ loved the church and gave himself up for her to make her holy, cleansing her by the washing with water through the word, and to present her to himself as a radiant church . . . In this same way, husbands ought to love their wives as their own bodies. He who loves his wife loves himself. After all, no one ever hated their own body, but they feed and care for their body, just as Christ does the church . . . Each one of you also must love his wife as he loves himself, and the wife must respect her husband.

COLOSSIANS 3:19

Husbands, love your wives and do not be harsh with them.

HOSEA 3:1

The LORD said to me, "Go, show your love to your wife again, though she is loved by another man and is an adulteress. Love her as the LORD loves the Israelites, though they turn to other gods and love the sacred raisin cakes."

1 CORINTHIANS 7:3–5

The husband should fulfill his marital duty to his wife, and likewise the wife to her husband . . . The husband does not have authority over his own body but yields it to his wife. Do not deprive each other except perhaps by mutual consent and for a time, so that you may devote yourselves to prayer. Then come together again so that Satan will not tempt you because of your lack of self-control.

MY ATTITUDE TOWARD SEX

GENESIS 1:27

So God created mankind in his own image, in the image of God he created them; male and female he created them.

GENESIS 2:24

That is why a man leaves his father and mother and is united to his wife, and they become one flesh.

1 TIMOTHY 4:4–5

For everything God created is good, and nothing is to be rejected if it is received with thanksgiving, because it is consecrated by the word of God and prayer.

HEBREWS 13:4

Marriage should be honored by all, and the marriage bed kept pure, for God will judge the adulterer and all the sexually immoral.

1 CORINTHIANS 7:4–5

The wife does not have authority over her own body but yields it to her husband. In the same way, the husband does not have authority over his own body but yields it to his wife. Do not deprive each other except perhaps by mutual consent and for a time, so that you may devote yourselves to prayer. Then come together again so that Satan will not tempt you because of your lack of self-control.

SONG OF SONGS 4:10–11,15

How delightful is your love, my sister, my bride! How much more pleasing is your love than wine, and the fragrance of your perfume more than any spice! Your lips drop sweetness as the honeycomb, my bride; milk and honey are under your tongue . . . You are a garden fountain, a well of flowing water streaming down from Lebanon.

SONG OF SONGS 7:6–8

How beautiful you are and how pleasing, my love, with your delights! Your stature is like that of the palm, and your breasts like clusters of fruit. I said, "I will climb the palm tree; I will take hold of its fruit." May your breasts be like clusters of grapes on the vine, the fragrance of your breath like apples.

———SEXUAL PRACTICES GOD FORBIDS———

EXODUS 20:14

"You shall not commit adultery."

ROMANS 1:26–27

Because of this, God gave them over to shameful lusts. Even their women exchanged natural sexual relations for unnatural ones. In the same way the men also abandoned natural relations with women and were inflamed with lust for one another. Men committed shameful acts with other men, and received in themselves the due penalty for their error.

LEVITICUS 18:6

"No one is to approach any close relative to have sexual relations. I am the LORD."

LEVITICUS 18:15–16

"Do not have sexual relations with your daughter-in-law. She is your son's wife; do not have relations with her. Do not have sexual relations with your brother's wife; that would dishonor your brother."

LEVITICUS 18:22–23

"Do not have sexual relations with a man as one does with a woman; that is detestable. Do not have sexual relations with an animal and defile yourself with it. A woman must not present herself to an animal to have sexual relations with it; that is a perversion."

DEUTERONOMY 23:17–18

No Israelite man or woman is to become a shrine prostitute. You must not bring the earnings of a female prostitute or of a male prostitute into the house of the LORD your God to pay any vow, because the LORD your God detests them both.

GALATIANS 5:19

The acts of the flesh are obvious: sexual immorality, impurity and debauchery.

_____MY APPROACH TO CONFLICT_____

2 TIMOTHY 2:24–25

And the Lord's servant must not be quarrelsome but must be kind to everyone, able to teach, not resentful. Opponents must be gently instructed, in the hope that God will grant them repentance leading them to a knowledge of the truth.

JAMES 3:17–18

But the wisdom that comes from heaven is first of all pure; then peace-loving, considerate, submissive, full of mercy and good fruit, impartial and sincere. Peacemakers who sow in peace reap a harvest of righteousness.

COLOSSIANS 3:16

Let the message of Christ dwell among you richly as you teach and admonish one another with all wisdom through psalms, hymns, and songs from the Spirit, singing to God with gratitude in your hearts.

PROVERBS 13:18

Whoever disregards discipline comes to poverty and shame, but whoever heeds correction is honored.

1 CORINTHIANS 3:3

You are still worldly. For since there is jealousy and quarreling among you, are you not worldly? Are you not acting like mere humans?

PHILIPPIANS 2:2

Then make my joy complete by being like-minded, having the same love, being one in spirit and of one mind.

JAMES 4:1–2

What causes fights and quarrels among you? Don't they come from your desires that battle within you? You desire but do not have, so you kill. You covet but you cannot get what you want, so you quarrel and fight. You do not have because you do not ask God.

—————————MY APPROACH TO HURT—————————

1 PETER 3:9

Do not repay evil with evil or insult with insult. On the contrary, repay evil with blessing, because to this you were called so that you may inherit a blessing.

GALATIANS 6:9

Let us not become weary in doing good, for at the proper time we will reap a harvest if we do not give up.

LUKE 6:31

"Do to others as you would have them do to you."

LUKE 6:38

"Give, and it will be given to you. A good measure, pressed down, shaken together and running over, will be poured into your lap. For with the measure you use, it will be measured to you."

1 THESSALONIANS 3:12

May the Lord make your love increase and overflow for each other and for everyone else, just as ours does for you.

MATTHEW 5:23–24

"Therefore, if you are offering your gift at the altar and there remember that your brother or sister has something against you, leave your gift there in front of the altar. First go and be reconciled to them; then come and offer your gift."

PSALM 37:5–6

Commit your way to the LORD; trust in him and he will do this: He will make your righteous reward shine like the dawn, your vindication like the noonday sun.

COLOSSIANS 3:13

Bear with each other and forgive one another if any of you has a grievance against someone. Forgive as the Lord forgave you.

_____MY APPROACH TO ANGER_____

PROVERBS 12:18

The words of the reckless pierce like swords, but the tongue of the wise brings healing.

PSALM 37:8

Refrain from anger and turn from wrath; do not fret — it leads only to evil.

ISAIAH 54:8

"In a surge of anger I hid my face from you for a moment, but with everlasting kindness I will have compassion on you," says the LORD your Redeemer.

ISAIAH 32:17

The fruit of that righteousness will be peace; its effect will be quietness and confidence forever.

MICAH 7:18–19

Who is a God like you, who pardons sin and forgives the transgression of the remnant of his inheritance? You do not stay angry forever but delight to show mercy. You will again have compassion on us; you will tread our sins underfoot and hurl all our iniquities into the depths of the sea.

LUKE 6:37

"Do not judge, and you will not be judged. Do not condemn, and you will not be condemned. Forgive, and you will be forgiven."

ISAIAH 12:1

In that day you will say: "I will praise you, LORD. Although you were angry with me, your anger has turned away and you have comforted me."

HEBREWS 12:14

Make every effort to live in peace with everyone and to be holy; without holiness no one will see the Lord.

_____MY APPROACH TO WEAKNESS_____

ISAIAH 30:18

Yet the LORD longs to be gracious to you; therefore he will rise up to show you compassion. For the LORD is a God of justice. Blessed are all who wait for him!

MATTHEW 7:3–4

"Why do you look at the speck of sawdust in your brother's eye and pay no attention to the plank in your own eye? How can you say to your brother, 'Let me take the speck out of your eye,' when all the time there is a plank in your own eye?"

ISAIAH 40:29

He gives strength to the weary and increases the power of the weak.

1 THESSALONIANS 5:11

Therefore encourage one another and build each other up, just as in fact you are doing.

MATTHEW 12:7

"If you had known what these words mean, 'I desire mercy, not sacrifice,' you would not have condemned the innocent."

MATTHEW 7:1–2

"Do not judge, or you too will be judged. For in the same way you judge others, you will be judged, and with the measure you use, it will be measured to you."

COLOSSIANS 3:12

Therefore, as God's chosen people, holy and dearly loved, clothe yourselves with compassion, kindness, humility, gentleness and patience.

ISAIAH 54:4

"Do not be afraid; you will not be put to shame. Do not fear disgrace; you will not be humiliated. You will forget the shame of your youth and remember no more the reproach of your widowhood."

_____MY ATTITUDE OF OPENNESS_____

EPHESIANS 4:15–16

Instead, speaking the truth in love, we will grow to become in every respect the mature body of him who is the head, that is, Christ. From him the whole body, joined and held together by every supporting ligament, grows and builds itself up in love, as each part does its work.

JAMES 5:16

Therefore confess your sins to each other and pray for each other so that you may be healed. The prayer of a righteous person is powerful and effective.

PSALM 101:7

No one who practices deceit will dwell in my house; no one who speaks falsely will stand in my presence.

2 CORINTHIANS 3:18

And we all, who with unveiled faces contemplate the Lord's glory, are being transformed into his image with ever-increasing glory, which comes from the Lord, who is the Spirit.

HEBREWS 4:13

Nothing in all creation is hidden from God's sight. Everything is uncovered and laid bare before the eyes of him to whom we must give account.

EPHESIANS 4:25

Therefore each of you must put off falsehood and speak truthfully to your neighbor, for we are all members of one body.

2 CORINTHIANS 6:11,13

We have spoken freely to you, Corinthians, and opened wide our hearts to you . . . open wide your hearts also.

_____MY ATTITUDE OF FORGIVENESS_____

LUKE 17:3–4

"If your brother or sister sins against you, rebuke them; and if they repent, forgive them. Even if they sin against you seven times in a day and seven times come back to you saying 'I repent,' you must forgive them."

PSALM 130:3–4

If you, LORD, kept a record of sins, Lord, who could stand? But with you there is forgiveness, so that we can, with reverence, serve you.

MATTHEW 6:14–15

For if you forgive other people when they sin against you, your heavenly Father will also forgive you. But if you do not forgive others their sins, your Father will not forgive your sins.

EPHESIANS 4:32

Be kind and compassionate to one another, forgiving each other, just as in Christ God forgave you.

LUKE 7:47

"Therefore, I tell you, her many sins have been forgiven — as her great love has shown. But whoever has been forgiven little loves little."

ISAIAH 30:15

This is what the Sovereign LORD, the Holy One of Israel, says: "In repentance and rest is your salvation, in quietness and trust is your strength, but you would have none of it."

COLOSSIANS 3:13

Bear with each other and forgive one another if any of you has a grievance against someone. Forgive as the Lord forgave you.

RELATIONSHIPS WITH MY CHILDREN

HOW TO FATHER

DEUTERONOMY 4:40

Keep his decrees and commands, which I am giving you today, so that it may go well with you and your children after you and that you may live long in the land the LORD your God gives you for all time.

DEUTERONOMY 4:9

Only be careful, and watch yourselves closely so that you do not forget the things your eyes have seen or let them fade from your heart as long as you live. Teach them to your children and to their children after them.

DEUTERONOMY 30:19–20

This day I call the heavens and the earth as witnesses against you that I have set before you life and death, blessings and curses. Now choose life, so that you and your children may live and that you may love the LORD your God, listen to his voice, and hold fast to him. For the LORD is your life, and he will give you many years in the land he swore to give to your fathers, Abraham, Isaac and Jacob.

TITUS 2:7

In everything set them an example by doing what is good. In your teaching show integrity, seriousness.

HEBREWS 10:35–36

So do not throw away your confidence; it will be richly rewarded. You need to persevere so that when you have done the will of God, you will receive what he has promised.

GENESIS 18:19

"For I have chosen him, so that he will direct his children and his household after him to keep the way of the LORD by doing what is right and just, so that the LORD will bring about for Abraham what he has promised him."

EPHESIANS 6:4

Fathers, do not exasperate your children; instead, bring them up in the training and instruction of the Lord.

_____MY GOALS IN CHILD REARING_____

1 THESSALONIANS 2:11–12

For you know that we dealt with each of you as a father deals with his own children, encouraging, comforting and urging you to live lives worthy of God, who calls you into his kingdom and glory.

PROVERBS 1:2–3

For gaining wisdom and instruction; for understanding words of insight; for receiving instruction in prudent behavior, doing what is right and just and fair.

MATTHEW 22:36–40

"Teacher, which is the greatest commandment in the Law?" Jesus replied: "'Love the Lord your God with all your heart and with all your soul and with all your mind.' This is the first and greatest commandment. And the second is like it: 'Love your neighbor as yourself.' All the Law and the Prophets hang on these two commandments."

EPHESIANS 5:1–2

Follow God's example, therefore, as dearly loved children . . . walk in the way of love, just as Christ loved us and gave himself up for us as a fragrant offering and sacrifice to God.

1 TIMOTHY 4:12

Don't let anyone look down on you because you are young, but set an example for the believers in speech, in conduct, in love, in faith and in purity.

2 TIMOTHY 3:15

And how from infancy you have known the Holy Scriptures, which are able to make you wise for salvation through faith in Christ Jesus.

_____MY PURPOSE IN DISCIPLINE_____

HEBREWS 12:10–11

They disciplined us for a little while as they thought best; but God disciplines us for our good, in order that we may share in his holiness. No discipline seems pleasant at the time, but painful. Later on, however, it produces a harvest of righteousness and peace for those who have been trained by it.

PROVERBS 3:11–12

My son, do not despise the LORD's discipline, and do not resent his rebuke, because the LORD disciplines those he loves, as a father the son he delights in.

PSALM 39:11

"When you rebuke and discipline anyone for their sin, you consume their wealth like a moth — surely everyone is but a breath."

PROVERBS 5:23

For lack of discipline they will die, led astray by their own great folly.

1 CORINTHIANS 11:32

Nevertheless, when we are judged in this way by the Lord, we are being disciplined so that we will not be finally condemned with the world.

PROVERBS 23:13

Do not withhold discipline from a child; if you punish them with the rod, they will not die.

PROVERBS 19:18

Discipline your children, for in that there is hope; do not be a willing party to their death.

2 TIMOTHY 3:16–17

All Scripture is God-breathed and is useful for teaching, rebuking, correcting and training in righteousness, so that the servant of God may be thoroughly equipped for every good work.

_____MY RESOURCES FOR DISCIPLINE_____

2 TIMOTHY 4:2

Preach the word; be prepared in season and out of season; correct, rebuke and encourage — with great patience and careful instruction.

PROVERBS 12:25

Anxiety weighs down the heart, but a kind word cheers it up.

LEVITICUS 19:17

"Do not hate a fellow Israelite in your heart. Rebuke your neighbor frankly so you will not share in their guilt."

PROVERBS 29:15

A rod and a reprimand impart wisdom, but a child left undisciplined disgraces its mother.

PROVERBS 22:15

Folly is bound up in the heart of a child, but the rod of discipline will drive it far away.

1 JOHN 1:9

If we confess our sins, he is faithful and just and will forgive us our sins and purify us from all unrighteousness.

2 CORINTHIANS 5:19

That God was reconciling the world to himself in Christ, not counting people's sins against them. And he has committed to us the message of reconciliation.

PROVERBS 22:6

Start children off on the way they should go, and even when they are old they will not turn from it.

1 CORINTHIANS 4:15–17

Even if you had ten thousand guardians in Christ, you do not have many fathers, for in Christ Jesus I became your father through the gospel. Therefore I urge you to imitate me . . . He will remind you of my way of life in Christ Jesus, which agrees with what I teach everywhere in every church.

_____PROMOTING SPIRITUAL GROWTH_____

PROVERBS 11:27

Whoever seeks good finds favor, but evil comes to one who searches for it.

ROMANS 14:13

Therefore let us stop passing judgment on one another. Instead, make up your mind not to put any stumbling block or obstacle in the way of a brother or sister.

PROVERBS 3:3–4

Let love and faithfulness never leave you; bind them around your neck, write them on the tablet of your heart. Then you will win favor and a good name in the sight of God and man.

DEUTERONOMY 29:29

The secret things belong to the LORD our God, but the things revealed belong to us and to our children forever, that we may follow all the words of this law.

HEBREWS 10:24–25

And let us consider how we may spur one another on toward love and good deeds, not giving up meeting together, as some are in the habit of doing, but encouraging one another — and all the more as you see the Day approaching.

DEUTERONOMY 6:5–7

Love the LORD your God with all your heart and with all your soul and with all your strength. These commandments that I give you today are to be on your hearts. Impress them on your children. Talk about them when you sit at home and when you walk along the road, when you lie down and when you get up.

_____PRAYING FOR MY CHILDREN_____

EPHESIANS 1:16–17

I have not stopped giving thanks for you, remembering you in my prayers. I keep asking that the God of our Lord Jesus Christ, the glorious Father, may give you the Spirit of wisdom and revelation, so that you may know him better.

EPHESIANS 1:18–19

I pray that the eyes of your heart may be enlightened in order that you may know the hope to which he has called you, the riches of his glorious inheritance in his holy people, and his incomparably great power for us who believe. That power is the same as the mighty strength.

EPHESIANS 3:16–17

I pray that out of his glorious riches he may strengthen you with power through his Spirit in your inner being, so that

Christ may dwell in your hearts through faith. And I pray that you, being rooted and established in love.

Ephesians 3:17–19

So that Christ may dwell in your hearts through faith. And I pray that you, being rooted and established in love, may have power, together with all the Lord's holy people, to grasp how wide and long and high and deep is the love of Christ, and to know this love that surpasses knowledge — that you may be filled to the measure of all the fullness of God.

Philippians 1:9–10

And this is my prayer: that your love may abound more and more in knowledge and depth of insight, so that you may be able to discern what is best and may be pure and blameless for the day of Christ.

_____COMMUNICATING LOVE_____

1 John 4:9–10

This is how God showed his love among us: He sent his one and only Son into the world that we might live through him. This is love: not that we loved God, but that he loved us and sent his Son as an atoning sacrifice for our sins.

1 John 3:18

Dear children, let us not love with words or speech but with actions and in truth.

1 Samuel 12:23

"As for me, far be it from me that I should sin against the Lord by failing to pray for you. And I will teach you the way that is good and right."

Psalm 89:33

"But I will not take my love from him, nor will I ever betray my faithfulness."

1 Kings 3:3

Solomon showed his love for the Lord by walking according to the instructions given him by his father David, except that he offered sacrifices and burned incense on the high places.

Nehemiah 9:17

"They refused to listen and failed to remember the miracles you performed among them. They became stiff-necked and in their rebellion appointed a leader in order to return to their slavery. But you are a forgiving God, gracious and compassionate, slow to anger and abounding in love. Therefore you did not desert them."

Hebrews 12:6

"Because the Lord disciplines the one he loves, and he chastens everyone he accepts as his son."

1 Corinthians 13:4–7

Love is patient, love is kind. It does not envy, it does not boast, it is not proud. It does not dishonor others, it is not self-seeking, it is not easily angered, it keeps no record of wrongs.

Love does not delight in evil but rejoices with the truth. It always protects, always trusts, always hopes, always perseveres.

_____TELLING MY CHILD ABOUT GOD_____

EXODUS 10:2

"That you may tell your children and grandchildren how I dealt harshly with the Egyptians and how I performed my signs among them . . . that you may know that I am the LORD."

EXODUS 12:26

"And when your children ask you, 'What does this ceremony mean to you?'"

DEUTERONOMY 6:5–7,9

Love the LORD your God with all your heart and with all your soul and with all your strength. These commandments that I give you today are to be on your hearts. Impress them on your children. Talk about them when you sit at home and when you walk along the road, when you lie down and when you get up . . . Write them on the doorframes of your houses and on your gates.

COLOSSIANS 3:16–17

Let the message of Christ dwell among you richly as you teach and admonish one another with all wisdom through psalms, hymns, and songs from the Spirit, singing to God with gratitude in your hearts. And whatever you do, whether in word or deed, do it all in the name of the Lord Jesus, giving thanks to God the Father through him.

DEUTERONOMY 4:9–10

Only be careful, and watch yourselves closely so that you do not forget the things your eyes have seen or let them fade from your heart as long as you live. Teach them to your children and to their children after them. Remember the day you stood before the LORD your God at Horeb, when he said to me, "Assemble the people before me to hear my words so that they may learn to revere me as long as they live in the land and may teach them to their children."

AVOIDING PROBLEM SITUATIONS

PROVERBS 10:12

Hatred stirs up conflict, but love covers over all wrongs.

PSALM 34:12–13

Whoever of you loves life and desires to see many good days, keep your tongue from evil and your lips from telling lies.

COLOSSIANS 3:8

But now you must also rid yourselves of all such things as these: anger, rage, malice, slander, and filthy language from your lips.

EXODUS 23:2

"Do not follow the crowd in doing wrong. When you give testimony in a lawsuit, do not pervert justice by siding with the crowd."

PROVERBS 1:10

My son, if sinful men entice you, do not give in to them.

EPHESIANS 6:1–3

Children, obey your parents in the Lord, for this is right. "Honor your father and mother" — which is the first commandment with a promise — "so that it may go well with you and that you may enjoy long life on the earth."

GALATIANS 6:4

Each one should test their own actions. Then they can take pride in themselves alone, without comparing themselves to someone else.

PHILIPPIANS 2:4

Not looking to your own interests but each of you to the interests of the others.

LEVITICUS 19:11

"Do not steal. Do not lie. Do not deceive one another."

PROVERBS 3:30

Do not accuse anyone for no reason — when they have done you no harm.

PROVERBS 15:1

A gentle answer turns away wrath, but a harsh word stirs up anger.

PROVERBS 18:13

To answer before listening — that is folly and shame.

PROVERBS 28:13

Whoever conceals their sins does not prosper, but the one who confesses and renounces them finds mercy.

PROVERBS 29:25

Fear of man will prove to be a snare, but whoever trusts in the LORD is kept safe.

MATTHEW 18:21–22

Then Peter came to Jesus and asked, "Lord, how many times shall I forgive my brother or sister who sins against me? Up to seven times?" Jesus answered, "I tell you, not seven times, but seventy-seven times."

1 CORINTHIANS 15:33

Do not be misled: "Bad company corrupts good character."

1 PETER 3:9

Do not repay evil with evil or insult with insult. On the contrary, repay evil with blessing, because to this you were called so that you may inherit a blessing.

PROVERBS 12:22

The LORD detests lying lips, but he delights in people who are trustworthy.

PROVERBS 17:9

Whoever would foster love covers over an offense, but whoever repeats the matter separates close friends.

RELATIONSHIPS AT CHURCH

—————RECOGNIZING A GOOD CHURCH———————

ACTS 2:42

They devoted themselves to the apostles' teaching and to fellowship, to the breaking of bread and to prayer.

PSALM 105:2–3

Sing to him, sing praise to him; tell of all his wonderful acts. Glory in his holy name; let the hearts of those who seek the LORD rejoice.

ACTS 2:46–47

Every day they continued to meet together in the temple courts. They broke bread in their homes and ate together with glad and sincere hearts, praising God and enjoying the favor of all the people. And the Lord added to their number daily those who were being saved.

HEBREWS 13:9

Do not be carried away by all kinds of strange teachings. It is good for our hearts to be strengthened by grace, not by eating ceremonial foods, which is of no benefit to those who do so.

JAMES 1:22

Do not merely listen to the word, and so deceive yourselves. Do what it says.

1 PETER 1:8–9

Though you have not seen him, you love him; and even though you do not see him now, you believe in him and are filled with an inexpressible and glorious joy, for you are receiving the end result of your faith, the salvation of your souls.

JAMES 1:27

Religion that God our Father accepts as pure and faultless is this: to look after orphans and widows in their distress and to keep oneself from being polluted by the world.

_____MY ROLE IN CHRIST'S BODY_____

ROMANS 12:1

Therefore, I urge you, brothers and sisters, in view of God's mercy, to offer your bodies as a living sacrifice, holy and pleasing to God — this is your true and proper worship.

HEBREWS 10:24–25

And let us consider how we may spur one another on toward love and good deeds, not giving up meeting together, as some are in the habit of doing, but encouraging one another — and all the more as you see the Day approaching.

1 CORINTHIANS 15:58

Therefore, my dear brothers and sisters, stand firm. Let nothing move you. Always give yourselves fully to the work of the Lord, because you know that your labor in the Lord is not in vain.

1 TIMOTHY 4:12

Don't let anyone look down on you because you are young, but set an example for the believers in speech, in conduct, in love, in faith and in purity.

HEBREWS 13:16

And do not forget to do good and to share with others, for with such sacrifices God is pleased.

ROMANS 15:14

I myself am convinced, my brothers and sisters, that you yourselves are full of goodness, filled with knowledge and competent to instruct one another.

1 TIMOTHY 2:8

Therefore I want the men everywhere to pray, lifting up holy hands without anger or disputing.

1 PETER 4:10

Each of you should use whatever gift you have received to serve others, as faithful stewards of God's grace in its various forms.

MY SPIRITUAL GIFTS

1 CORINTHIANS 12:7,11

Now to each one the manifestation of the Spirit is given for the common good . . . All these are the work of one and the same Spirit, and he distributes them to each one, just as he determines.

ROMANS 1:11–12

I long to see you so that I may impart to you some spiritual gift to make you strong — that is, that you and I may be mutually encouraged by each other's faith.

ACTS 2:18

"Even on my servants, both men and women, I will pour out my Spirit in those days, and they will prophesy."

1 PETER 4:10–11

Each of you should use whatever gift you have received to serve others, as faithful stewards of God's grace in its various forms. If anyone speaks, they should do so as one who speaks the very words of God. If anyone serves, they should do so with the strength God provides, so that in all things God may be praised through Jesus Christ. To him be the glory and the power for ever and ever. Amen.

TITUS 3:8

This is a trustworthy saying. And I want you to stress these things, so that those who have trusted in God may be careful to devote themselves to doing what is good. These things are excellent and profitable for everyone.

EPHESIANS 6:7–8

Serve wholeheartedly, as if you were serving the Lord, not people, because you know that the Lord will reward each one for whatever good they do, whether they are slave or free.

_____MY FELLOWSHIP WITH OTHERS_____

ROMANS 12:16

Live in harmony with one another. Do not be proud, but be willing to associate with people of low position. Do not be conceited.

MATTHEW 18:19–20

"Again, truly I tell you that if two of you on earth agree about anything they ask for, it will be done for them by my Father in heaven. For where two or three gather in my name, there am I with them."

1 JOHN 1:7

But if we walk in the light, as he is in the light, we have fellowship with one another, and the blood of Jesus, his Son, purifies us from all sin.

ROMANS 12:18

If it is possible, as far as it depends on you, live at peace with everyone.

ROMANS 15:5–6

May the God who gives endurance and encouragement give you the same attitude of mind toward each other that Christ Jesus had, so that with one mind and one voice you may glorify the God and Father of our Lord Jesus Christ.

ROMANS 16:17

I urge you, brothers and sisters, to watch out for those who cause divisions and put obstacles in your way that are contrary to the teaching you have learned. Keep away from them.

1 PETER 3:8

Finally, all of you, be like-minded, be sympathetic, love one another, be compassionate and humble.

_____MY GIVING_____

ROMANS 12:13

Share with the Lord's people who are in need. Practice hospitality.

1 JOHN 3:17–18

If anyone has material possessions and sees a brother or sister in need but has no pity on them, how can the love of God be in that person? Dear children, let us not love with words or speech but with actions and in truth.

2 CORINTHIANS 8:13–14

Our desire is not that others might be relieved while you are hard pressed, but that there might be equality. At the present time your plenty will supply what they need, so that in turn their plenty will supply what you need. The goal is equality.

2 CORINTHIANS 9:6

Remember this: Whoever sows sparingly will also reap sparingly, and whoever sows generously will also reap generously.

2 CORINTHIANS 9:7

Each of you should give what you have decided in your heart to give, not reluctantly or under compulsion, for God loves a cheerful giver.

2 CORINTHIANS 9:10–11

Now he who supplies seed to the sower and bread for food will also supply and increase your store of seed and will enlarge the harvest of your righteousness. You will be enriched in every way so that you can be generous on every occasion, and through us your generosity will result in thanksgiving to God.

_____MY ATTITUDES TOWARD OTHERS_____

ROMANS 12:10

Be devoted to one another in love. Honor one another above yourselves.

1 TIMOTHY 5:1–2

Do not rebuke an older man harshly, but exhort him as if he were your father. Treat younger men as brothers, older women as mothers, and younger women as sisters, with absolute purity.

ROMANS 14:1

Accept the one whose faith is weak, without quarreling over disputable matters.

1 CORINTHIANS 5:11,13

But now I am writing to you that you must not associate with anyone who claims to be a brother or sister but is sexually immoral or greedy, an idolater or slanderer, a drunkard or swindler. Do not even eat with such people . . . God will judge those outside. "Expel the wicked person from among you."

ROMANS 14:3–4

The one who eats everything must not treat with contempt the one who does not, and the one who does not eat everything must not judge the one who does, for God has accepted them. Who are you to judge someone else's servant? To their own master, servants stand or fall. And they will stand, for the Lord is able to make them stand.

1 Thessalonians 5:14

And we urge you, brothers and sisters, warn those who are idle and disruptive, encourage the disheartened, help the weak, be patient with everyone.

BEING A LEADER

Isaiah 40:11

He tends his flock like a shepherd: He gathers the lambs in his arms and carries them close to his heart; he gently leads those that have young.

Matthew 20:25–28

Jesus called them together and said, "You know that the rulers of the Gentiles lord it over them, and their high officials exercise authority over them. Not so with you. Instead, whoever wants to become great among you must be your servant, and whoever wants to be first must be your slave — just as the Son of Man did not come to be served, but to serve, and to give his life as a ransom for many."

1 Timothy 3:8–10

In the same way, [leaders] are to be worthy of respect, sincere, not indulging in much wine, and not pursuing dishonest gain. They must keep hold of the deep truths of the faith with a clear conscience. They must first be tested; and then if there is nothing against them, let them serve as deacons.

EZEKIEL 34:15–16

"I myself will tend my sheep and have them lie down, declares the Sovereign LORD. I will search for the lost and bring back the strays. I will bind up the injured and strengthen the weak, but the sleek and the strong I will destroy. I will shepherd the flock with justice."

PROVERBS 15:33

Wisdom's instruction is to fear the LORD, and humility comes before honor.

RELATING TO LEADERS

1 THESSALONIANS 5:12–13

Now we ask you, brothers and sisters, to acknowledge those who work hard among you, who care for you in the Lord and who admonish you. Hold them in the highest regard in love because of their work. Live in peace with each other.

1 TIMOTHY 5:19–20

Do not entertain an accusation against an elder unless it is brought by two or three witnesses. But those elders who are sinning you are to reprove before everyone, so that the others may take warning.

HEBREWS 13:7

Remember your leaders, who spoke the word of God to you. Consider the outcome of their way of life and imitate their faith.

1 PETER 5:5–6

In the same way, you who are younger, submit yourselves to your elders. All of you, clothe yourselves with humility toward one another, because, "God opposes the proud but shows favor to the humble." Humble yourselves, therefore, under God's mighty hand, that he may lift you up in due time.

HEBREWS 13:17

Have confidence in your leaders and submit to their authority, because they keep watch over you as those who must give an account. Do this so that their work will be a joy, not a burden, for that would be of no benefit to you.

MATTHEW 18:4

"Therefore, whoever takes the lowly position of this child is the greatest in the kingdom of heaven."

ENRICHING MY RELATIONSHIPS

TITUS 3:10

Warn a divisive person once, and then warn them a second time. After that, have nothing to do with them.

ROMANS 12:17

Do not repay anyone evil for evil. Be careful to do what is right in the eyes of everyone.

EPHESIANS 6:18

And pray in the Spirit on all occasions with all kinds of prayers and requests. With this in mind, be alert and always keep on praying for all the Lord's people.

EXODUS 22:25

"If you lend money to one of my people among you who is needy, do not treat it like a business deal; charge no interest."

2 CORINTHIANS 4:2

Rather, we have renounced secret and shameful ways; we do not use deception, nor do we distort the word of God. On the contrary, by setting forth the truth plainly we commend ourselves to everyone's conscience in the sight of God.

PROVERBS 28:13

Whoever conceals their sins does not prosper, but the one who confesses and renounces them finds mercy.

PROVERBS 27:5

Better is open rebuke than hidden love.

COLOSSIANS 3:9–10

Do not lie to each other, since you have taken off your old self with its practices and have put on the new self, which is being renewed . . . in the image of its Creator.

PHILIPPIANS 4:5

Let your gentleness be evident to all. The Lord is near.

ROMANS 15:7

Accept one another, then, just as Christ accepted you, in order to bring praise to God.

ROMANS 15:2

Each of us should please our neighbors for their good, to build them up.

1 Corinthians 4:3–5

I care very little if I am judged by you or by any human court; indeed, I do not even judge myself. My conscience is clear, but that does not make me innocent. It is the Lord who judges me. Therefore judge nothing before the appointed time; wait until the Lord comes. He will bring to light what is hidden in darkness and will expose the motives of the heart. At that time each will receive their praise from God.

Psalm 37:37

Consider the blameless, observe the upright; a future awaits those who seek peace.

1 Peter 3:8

Finally, all of you, be like-minded, be sympathetic, love one another, be compassionate and humble.

1 Corinthians 6:4

Therefore, if you have disputes about such matters, do you ask for a ruling from those whose way of life is scorned in the church?

Proverbs 17:9

Whoever would foster love covers over an offense, but whoever repeats the matter separates close friends.

RELATIONSHIPS IN THE WORLD

———HOW CHRISTIAN VALUES DIFFER———

DEUTERONOMY 4:39

Acknowledge and take to heart this day that the LORD is God in heaven above and on the earth below. There is no other.

1 TIMOTHY 6:11

But you, man of God . . . pursue righteousness, godliness, faith, love, endurance and gentleness.

LUKE 16:15

He said to them, "You are the ones who justify yourselves in the eyes of others, but God knows your hearts. What people value highly is detestable in God's sight."

DEUTERONOMY 10:12

And now, Israel, what does the LORD your God ask of you but to fear the LORD your God, to walk in obedience to him, to love him, to serve the LORD your God with all your heart and with all your soul.

PHILIPPIANS 3:10

I want to know Christ — yes, to know the power of his resurrection and participation in his sufferings, becoming like him in his death.

PHILIPPIANS 3:8

What is more, I consider everything a loss because of the surpassing worth of knowing Christ Jesus my Lord, for whose sake I have lost all things. I consider them garbage, that I may gain Christ.

2 TIMOTHY 2:3–5

Join with me in suffering, like a good soldier of Christ Jesus. No one serving as a soldier gets entangled in civilian affairs, but rather tries to please his commanding officer. Similarly, anyone who competes as an athlete does not receive the victor's crown except by competing according to the rules.

RESPONDING TO THE WORLD

1 JOHN 2:15–16

Do not love the world or anything in the world. If anyone loves the world, love for the Father is not in them. For everything in the world — the lust of the flesh, the lust of the eyes, and the pride of life — comes not from the Father but from the world.

ROMANS 12:2

Do not conform to the pattern of this world, but be transformed by the renewing of your mind. Then you will be able to test and approve what God's will is — his good, pleasing and perfect will.

MATTHEW 6:19–21

"Do not store up for yourselves treasures on earth, where moths and vermin destroy, and where thieves break in and steal. But store up for yourselves treasures in heaven, where moths and vermin do not destroy, and where thieves do not break in and steal. For where your treasure is, there your heart will be also."

1 JOHN 2:17

The world and its desires pass away, but whoever does the will of God lives forever.

1 CORINTHIANS 1:28

God chose the lowly things of this world and the despised things — and the things that are not — to nullify the things that are.

RESPONDING TO UNBELIEVERS

ROMANS 13:8

Let no debt remain outstanding, except the continuing debt to love one another, for whoever loves others has fulfilled the law.

2 CORINTHIANS 6:14

Do not be yoked together with unbelievers. For what do righteousness and wickedness have in common? Or what fellowship can light have with darkness?

ISAIAH 51:7

"Hear me, you who know what is right, you people who have taken my instruction to heart: Do not fear the reproach of mere mortals or be terrified by their insults."

1 CORINTHIANS 5:9–10

I wrote to you in my letter not to associate with sexually immoral people — not at all meaning the people of this world who are immoral, or the greedy and swindlers, or idolaters. In that case you would have to leave this world.

PSALM 49:16–17

Do not be overawed when others grow rich, when the splendor of their houses increases; for they will take nothing with them when they die, their splendor will not descend with them.

ROMANS 13:7

Give to everyone what you owe them: If you owe taxes, pay taxes; if revenue, then revenue; if respect, then respect; if honor, then honor.

MATTHEW 9:13

"But go and learn what this means: 'I desire mercy, not sacrifice.' For I have not come to call the righteous, but sinners."

RELATING TO UNBELIEVERS

JAMES 2:8–9

If you really keep the royal law found in Scripture, "Love your neighbor as yourself," you are doing right. But if you show favoritism, you sin and are convicted by the law as lawbreakers.

MATTHEW 5:16

"In the same way, let your light shine before others, that they may see your good deeds and glorify your Father in heaven."

1 PETER 3:14–15

But even if you should suffer for what is right, you are blessed. "Do not fear their threats; do not be frightened." But in your hearts revere Christ as Lord. Always be prepared to give an answer to everyone who asks you to give the reason for the hope that you have. But do this with gentleness and respect.

LUKE 6:35–36

"But love your enemies, do good to them, and lend to them without expecting to get anything back. Then your reward will be great, and you will be children of the Most High, because he is kind to the ungrateful and wicked. Be merciful, just as your Father is merciful."

2 TIMOTHY 2:23–24

Don't have anything to do with foolish and stupid arguments, because you know they produce quarrels. And the Lord's servant must not be quarrelsome but must be kind to everyone, able to teach, not resentful.

1 PETER 2:12

Live such good lives among the pagans that, though they accuse you of doing wrong, they may see your good deeds and glorify God on the day he visits us.

RESPONDING TO MATERIALISM

PHILIPPIANS 4:12–13

I know what it is to be in need, and I know what it is to have plenty. I have learned the secret of being content in any and every situation, whether well fed or hungry, whether living in plenty or in want. I can do all this through him who gives me strength.

DEUTERONOMY 8:11–14

Be careful that you do not forget the LORD your God, failing to observe his commands, his laws and his decrees that I am giving you this day. Otherwise, when you eat and are satisfied, when you build fine houses and settle down, and when your herds and flocks grow large and your silver and gold increase and all you have is multiplied, then your heart will become proud and you will forget the LORD your God, who brought you out of Egypt, out of the land of slavery.

1 TIMOTHY 6:6–8

But godliness with contentment is great gain. For we brought nothing into the world, and we can take nothing out of it. But if we have food and clothing, we will be content with that.

MATTHEW 6:31–33

"So do not worry, saying, 'What shall we eat?' or 'What shall we drink?' or 'What shall we wear?' For the pagans run after all these things, and your heavenly Father knows that you need them. But seek first his kingdom and his righteousness, and all these things will be given to you as well."

RESPONSIBILITIES AS A CITIZEN

1 PETER 2:13–14

Submit yourselves for the Lord's sake to every human authority: whether to the emperor, as the supreme authority, or to governors, who are sent by him to punish those who do wrong and to commend those who do right.

ROMANS 13:1

Let everyone be subject to the governing authorities, for there is no authority except that which God has established. The authorities that exist have been established by God.

ROMANS 13:3–5

For rulers hold no terror for those who do right, but for those who do wrong. Do you want to be free from fear of the one in authority? Then do what is right and you will be commended. For the one in authority is God's servant for your good. But if you do wrong, be afraid, for rulers do not bear the sword for no reason . . . Therefore, it is necessary to submit to the authorities, not only because of possible punishment but also as a matter of conscience.

TITUS 3:1

Remind the people to be subject to rulers and authorities, to be obedient, to be ready to do whatever is good.

1 TIMOTHY 2:1–2

I urge, then, first of all, that petitions, prayers, intercession and thanksgiving be made for all people — for kings and all those in authority, that we may live peaceful and quiet lives in all godliness and holiness.

_____RESPONSIBILITIES TO THE POOR_____

PROVERBS 21:13

Whoever shuts their ears to the cry of the poor will also cry out and not be answered.

ISAIAH 10:1–2

Woe to those who make unjust laws, to those who issue oppressive decrees, to deprive the poor of their rights and withhold justice from the oppressed of my people, making widows their prey and robbing the fatherless.

ISAIAH 58:6–8

"Is not this the kind of fasting I have chosen: to loose the chains of injustice and untie the cords of the yoke, to set the oppressed free and break every yoke? Is it not to share your food with the hungry and to provide the poor wanderer with shelter — when you see the naked, to clothe them, and not to turn away from your own flesh and blood? Then your light will break forth like the dawn, and your healing will quickly appear; then your righteousness will go before you, and the glory of the LORD will be your rear guard."

DEUTERONOMY 15:11

There will always be poor people in the land. Therefore I command you to be openhanded toward your fellow Israelites who are poor and needy in your land.

GALATIANS 2:10

All they asked was that we should continue to remember the poor, the very thing I had been eager to do all along.

PSALM 82:2–4

"How long will you defend the unjust and show partiality to the wicked? Defend the weak and the fatherless; uphold the cause of the poor and the oppressed. Rescue the weak and the needy; deliver them from the hand of the wicked."

PROVERBS 22:9

The generous will themselves be blessed, for they share their food with the poor.

—————RESPONSIBILITIES TO OTHERS—————

DEUTERONOMY 1:17

"Do not show partiality in judging; hear both small and great alike. Do not be afraid of anyone, for judgment belongs to God. Bring me any case too hard for you, and I will hear it."

PHILEMON 6

I pray that your partnership with us in the faith may be effective in deepening your understanding of every good thing we share for the sake of Christ.

MICAH 6:8

He has shown you, O mortal, what is good. And what does the LORD require of you? To act justly and to love mercy and to walk humbly with your God.

HEBREWS 13:3

Continue to remember those in prison as if you were together with them in prison, and those who are mistreated as if you yourselves were suffering.

LEVITICUS 19:18

"Do not seek revenge or bear a grudge against anyone among your people, but love your neighbor as yourself. I am the LORD."

HEBREWS 13:2

Do not forget to show hospitality to strangers, for by so doing some people have shown hospitality to angels without knowing it.

ROMANS 12:21

Do not be overcome by evil, but overcome evil with good.

LEVITICUS 19:16

"Do not go about spreading slander among your people. Do not do anything that endangers your neighbor's life. I am the LORD."

LUKE 6:27–28

"But to you who are listening I say: Love your enemies, do good to those who hate you, bless those who curse you, pray for those who mistreat you."

_____INTRODUCING A PERSON TO JESUS_____

2 TIMOTHY 1:8

So do not be ashamed of the testimony about our Lord or of me his prisoner. Rather, join with me in suffering for the gospel, by the power of God.

ISAIAH 59:1–2

Surely the arm of the LORD is not too short to save, nor his ear too dull to hear. But your iniquities have separated you from your God; your sins have hidden his face from you, so that he will not hear.

JOHN 3:16

For God so loved the world that he gave his one and only Son, that whoever believes in him shall not perish but have eternal life.

JOHN 11:25–26

Jesus said to her, "I am the resurrection and the life. The one who believes in me will live, even though they die; and whoever lives by believing in me will never die. Do you believe this?"

EPHESIANS 2:8–9

For it is by grace you have been saved, through faith — and this is not from yourselves, it is the gift of God — not by works, so that no one can boast.

1 PETER 3:15–16

But in your hearts revere Christ as Lord. Always be prepared to give an answer to everyone who asks you to give the reason for the hope that you have. But do this with gentleness and respect, keeping a clear conscience, so that those who speak maliciously against your good behavior in Christ may be ashamed of their slander.

ACTS 8:4

Those who had been scattered preached the word wherever they went.

_____MY ATTITUDE TOWARD MONEY_____

PROVERBS 16:8

Better a little with righteousness than much gain with injustice.

1 TIMOTHY 6:9–10

Those who want to get rich fall into temptation and a trap and into many foolish and harmful desires that plunge people into ruin and destruction. For the love of money is a root of all kinds of evil. Some people, eager for money, have wandered from the faith and pierced themselves with many griefs.

MATTHEW 6:24

"No one can serve two masters. Either you will hate the one and love the other, or you will be devoted to the one and despise the other. You cannot serve both God and money."

PROVERBS 3:9–10

Honor the LORD with your wealth, with the firstfruits of all your crops; then your barns will be filled to overflowing, and your vats will brim over with new wine.

DEUTERONOMY 8:18

But remember the LORD your God, for it is he who gives you the ability to produce wealth, and so confirms his covenant, which he swore to your ancestors, as it is today.

1 TIMOTHY 6:17–18

Command those who are rich in this present world not to be arrogant nor to put their hope in wealth, which is so uncertain, but to put their hope in God, who richly provides us with everything for our enjoyment. Command them to do good, to be rich in good deeds, and to be generous and willing to share.

MY ATTITUDE TOWARD WORK

TITUS 3:14

Our people must learn to devote themselves to doing what is good, in order to provide for urgent needs and not live unproductive lives.

1 THESSALONIANS 4:11–12

And to make it your ambition to lead a quiet life: You should mind your own business and work with your hands, just as we told you, so that your daily life may win the respect of outsiders and so that you will not be dependent on anybody.

2 THESSALONIANS 3:6–10

In the name of the Lord Jesus Christ, we command you, brothers and sisters, to keep away from every believer who is idle and disruptive and does not live according to the teaching you received from us. For you yourselves know how you ought to follow our example. We were not idle when we were with you, nor did we eat anyone's food without paying for it. On the contrary, we worked night and day, laboring and toiling so that we would not be a burden to any of you. We did this, not because we do not have the right to such help, but in order to offer ourselves as a model for you to imitate. For even when we were with you, we gave you this rule: "The one who is unwilling to work shall not eat."

PROVERBS 28:19

Those who work their land will have abundant food, but those who chase fantasies will have their fill of poverty.

PROVERBS 14:23

All hard work brings a profit, but mere talk leads only to poverty.

PART THREE

MY INNER LIFE AS A CHRISTIAN MAN

Strength to live successfully in your significant personal relationships comes from God's work within you. How good that his Word shows us how to be strengthened "with power through his Spirit in your inner being" (Ephesians 3:16). Through Christ and the resources he has provided, you can continue to grow toward your goal of Christian manhood.

UNDERSTANDING SCRIPTURE

1 JOHN 2:5

But if anyone obeys his word, love for God is truly made complete in them. This is how we know we are in him.

PSALM 19:7–9

The law of the LORD is perfect, refreshing the soul. The statutes of the LORD are trustworthy, making wise the simple. The precepts of the LORD are right, giving joy to the heart. The commands of the LORD are radiant, giving light to the eyes. The fear of the LORD is pure, enduring forever. The decrees of the LORD are firm, and all of them are righteous.

JEREMIAH 6:16

This is what the LORD says: "Stand at the crossroads and look; ask for the ancient paths, ask where the good way is, and walk in it, and you will find rest for your souls. But you said, 'We will not walk in it.'"

JAMES 1:25

But whoever looks intently into the perfect law that gives freedom, and continues in it — not forgetting what they have heard, but doing it — they will be blessed in what they do.

MATTHEW 7:24–25

"Therefore everyone who hears these words of mine and puts them into practice is like a wise man who built his house on the rock. The rain came down, the streams rose, and the winds blew and beat against that house; yet it did not fall, because it had its foundation on the rock."

LUKE 6:46

"Why do you call me, 'Lord, Lord,' and do not do what I say?"

JOHN 8:31–32

To the Jews who had believed him, Jesus said, "If you hold to my teaching, you are really my disciples. Then you will know the truth, and the truth will set you free."

DEVELOPING A PRAYER LIFE

PSALM 62:8

Trust in him at all times, you people; pour out your hearts to him, for God is our refuge.

PSALM 5:2–3

Hear my cry for help, my King and my God, for to you I pray. In the morning, LORD, you hear my voice; in the morning I lay my requests before you and wait expectantly.

COLOSSIANS 3:17

And whatever you do, whether in word or deed, do it all in the name of the Lord Jesus, giving thanks to God the Father through him.

PSALM 107:1

Give thanks to the LORD, for he is good; his love endures forever.

1 THESSALONIANS 5:16–18

Rejoice always, pray continually, give thanks in all circumstances; for this is God's will for you in Christ Jesus.

LUKE 11:9–10

"So I say to you: Ask and it will be given to you; seek and you will find; knock and the door will be opened to you. For everyone who asks receives; the one who seeks finds; and to the one who knocks, the door will be opened."

PSALM 18:6

In my distress I called to the LORD; I cried to my God for help. From his temple he heard my voice; my cry came before him, into his ears.

ISAIAH 65:24

"Before they call I will answer; while they are still speaking I will hear."

DEVELOPING A PRAISE LIFE

PSALM 63:4

I will praise you as long as I live, and in your name I will lift up my hands.

PSALM 70:4

But may all who seek you rejoice and be glad in you; may those who long for your saving help always say, "The LORD is great!"

ISAIAH 25:1

LORD, you are my God; I will exalt you and praise your name, for in perfect faithfulness you have done wonderful things, things planned long ago.

HEBREWS 13:15

Through Jesus, therefore, let us continually offer to God a sacrifice of praise — the fruit of lips that openly profess his name.

JEREMIAH 10:6–7

No one is like you, LORD; you are great, and your name is mighty in power. Who should not fear you, King of the nations? This is your due. Among all the wise leaders of the nations and in all their kingdoms, there is no one like you.

PSALM 13:5–6

But I trust in your unfailing love; my heart rejoices in your salvation. I will sing the LORD's praise, for he has been good to me.

PSALM 29:1–2

Ascribe to the LORD, you heavenly beings, ascribe to the LORD glory and strength. Ascribe to the LORD the glory due his name; worship the LORD in the splendor of his holiness.

_____OVERCOMING TEMPTATIONS_____

1 CORINTHIANS 10:13

No temptation has overtaken you except what is common to mankind. And God is faithful; he will not let you be tempted beyond what you can bear. But when you are tempted, he will also provide a way out so that you can endure it.

JAMES 1:5

If any of you lacks wisdom, you should ask God, who gives generously to all without finding fault, and it will be given to you.

JAMES 1:13–14

When tempted, no one should say, "God is tempting me." For God cannot be tempted by evil, nor does he tempt anyone; but each person is tempted when they are dragged away by their own evil desire and enticed.

2 TIMOTHY 2:22

Flee the evil desires of youth and pursue righteousness, faith, love and peace, along with those who call on the Lord out of a pure heart.

ISAIAH 7:7,9

Yet this is what the Sovereign LORD says: "'It will not take place, it will not happen . . . The head of Ephraim is Samaria, and the head of Samaria is only Remaliah's son. If you do not stand firm in your faith, you will not stand at all.'"

JAMES 1:2–4

Consider it pure joy, my brothers and sisters, whenever you face trials of many kinds, because you know that the testing of your faith produces perseverance. Let perseverance finish its work so that you may be mature and complete, not lacking anything.

_____LIVING AS A SINGLE_____

1 CORINTHIANS 7:8–9

Now to the unmarried and the widows I say: It is good for them to stay unmarried, as I do. But if they cannot control themselves, they should marry, for it is better to marry than to burn with passion.

1 CORINTHIANS 7:32–34

I would like you to be free from concern. An unmarried man is concerned about the Lord's affairs — how he can please the Lord. But a married man is concerned about the affairs of this world — how he can please his wife — and his interests are divided. An unmarried woman or virgin is concerned about the Lord's affairs: Her aim is to be devoted to the Lord in both body and spirit. But a married woman is concerned about the affairs of this world — how she can please her husband.

1 CORINTHIANS 7:38

So then, he who marries the virgin does right, but he who does not marry her does better.

ROMANS 8:28

And we know that in all things God works for the good of those who love him, who have been called according to his purpose.

HEBREWS 10:24–25

And let us consider how we may spur one another on toward love and good deeds, not giving up meeting together, as some are in the habit of doing, but encouraging one another — and all the more as you see the Day approaching.

ROMANS 12:13

Share with the Lord's people who are in need. Practice hospitality.

ROMANS 12:5

So in Christ we, though many, form one body, and each member belongs to all the others.

_____DEALING WITH PRIDE_____

JEREMIAH 9:23–24

This is what the LORD says: "Let not the wise boast of their wisdom or the strong boast of their strength or the rich boast of their riches, but let the one who boasts boast about this: that they have the understanding to know me, that I am the LORD, who exercises kindness, justice and righteousness on earth, for in these I delight," declares the LORD.

PSALM 19:12

But who can discern their own errors? Forgive my hidden faults.

JEREMIAH 17:5,7

This is what the LORD says: "Cursed is the one who trusts in man, who draws strength from mere flesh and whose heart turns away from the LORD . . . But blessed is the one who trusts in the LORD, whose confidence is in him."

1 CORINTHIANS 4:7

For who makes you different from anyone else? What do you have that you did not receive? And if you did receive it, why do you boast as though you did not?

1 SAMUEL 2:3

"Do not keep talking so proudly or let your mouth speak such arrogance, for the LORD is a God who knows, and by him deeds are weighed."

ISAIAH 2:17

The arrogance of man will be brought low and human pride humbled; the LORD alone will be exalted in that day.

2 CORINTHIANS 10:18

For it is not the one who commends himself who is approved, but the one whom the Lord commends.

_____DEALING WITH SELF-DOUBT_____

PSALM 147:10–11

His pleasure is not in the strength of the horse, nor his delight in the legs of the warrior; the LORD delights in those who fear him, who put their hope in his unfailing love.

ISAIAH 33:6

He will be the sure foundation for your times, a rich store of salvation and wisdom and knowledge; the fear of the LORD is the key to this treasure.

2 CORINTHIANS 12:9

But he said to me, "My grace is sufficient for you, for my power is made perfect in weakness." Therefore I will boast all the more gladly about my weaknesses, so that Christ's power may rest on me.

Isaiah 58:11

"The LORD will guide you always; he will satisfy your needs in a sun-scorched land and will strengthen your frame. You will be like a well-watered garden, like a spring whose waters never fail."

Psalm 27:13–14

I remain confident of this: I will see the goodness of the LORD in the land of the living. Wait for the LORD; be strong and take heart and wait for the LORD.

Luke 12:24

"Consider the ravens: They do not sow or reap, they have no storeroom or barn; yet God feeds them. And how much more valuable you are than birds!"

2 Thessalonians 2:16–17

May our Lord Jesus Christ himself and God our Father, who loved us and by his grace gave us eternal encouragement and good hope, encourage your hearts and strengthen you in every good deed and word.

_____DEALING WITH LONELINESS_____

1 Peter 4:9

Offer hospitality to one another without grumbling.

Romans 12:15

Rejoice with those who rejoice; mourn with those who mourn.

GALATIANS 5:13

You, my brothers and sisters, were called to be free. But do not use your freedom to indulge the flesh; rather, serve one another humbly in love.

PSALM 68:6

God sets the lonely in families, he leads out the prisoners with singing; but the rebellious live in a sun-scorched land.

LUKE 14:12–14

Then Jesus said to his host, "When you give a luncheon or dinner, do not invite your friends, your brothers or sisters, your relatives, or your rich neighbors; if you do, they may invite you back and so you will be repaid. But when you give a banquet, invite the poor, the crippled, the lame, the blind, and you will be blessed. Although they cannot repay you, you will be repaid at the resurrection of the righteous."

PROVERBS 24:1

Do not envy the wicked, do not desire their company.

HEBREWS 10:24–25

And let us consider how we may spur one another on toward love and good deeds, not giving up meeting together, as some are in the habit of doing, but encouraging one another — and all the more as you see the Day approaching.

ROMANS 14:1

Accept the one whose faith is weak, without quarreling over disputable matters.

——DEALING WITH DISCOURAGEMENT——

PSALM 42:11

Why, my soul, are you downcast? Why so disturbed within me? Put your hope in God, for I will yet praise him, my Savior and my God.

PSALM 31:7

I will be glad and rejoice in your love, for you saw my affliction and knew the anguish of my soul.

EPHESIANS 1:18–19

I pray that the eyes of your heart may be enlightened in order that you may know the hope to which he has called you, the riches of his glorious inheritance in his holy people, and his incomparably great power for us who believe. That power is the same as the mighty strength.

2 PETER 1:5–8

For this very reason, make every effort to add to your faith goodness; and to goodness, knowledge; and to knowledge, self-control; and to self-control, perseverance; and to perseverance, godliness; and to godliness, mutual affection; and to mutual affection, love. For if you possess these qualities in increasing measure, they will keep you from being ineffective and unproductive in your knowledge of our Lord Jesus Christ.

ISAIAH 40:30–31

Even youths grow tired and weary, and young men stumble and fall; but those who hope in the LORD will renew their strength. They will soar on wings like eagles; they will run and not grow weary, they will walk and not be faint.

_____CHANNELING MY THOUGHT LIFE_____

PHILIPPIANS 4:8

Finally, brothers and sisters, whatever is true, whatever is noble, whatever is right, whatever is pure, whatever is lovely, whatever is admirable — if anything is excellent or praiseworthy — think about such things.

ISAIAH 26:3

You will keep in perfect peace those whose minds are steadfast, because they trust in you.

ISAIAH 55:7

Let the wicked forsake their ways and the unrighteous their thoughts. Let them turn to the LORD, and he will have mercy on them, and to our God, for he will freely pardon.

TITUS 1:15

To the pure, all things are pure, but to those who are corrupted and do not believe, nothing is pure. In fact, both their minds and consciences are corrupted.

PSALM 119:37

Turn my eyes away from worthless things; preserve my life according to your word.

HEBREWS 4:12–13

For the word of God is alive and active. Sharper than any double-edged sword, it penetrates even to dividing soul and spirit, joints and marrow; it judges the thoughts and attitudes of the heart. Nothing in all creation is hidden from God's sight. Everything is uncovered and laid bare before the eyes of him to whom we must give account.

ROMANS 12:2

Do not conform to the pattern of this world, but be transformed by the renewing of your mind. Then you will be able to test and approve what God's will is — his good, pleasing and perfect will.

_____DEALING WITH WORRY_____

ISAIAH 54:10

"Though the mountains be shaken and the hills be removed, yet my unfailing love for you will not be shaken nor my covenant of peace be removed," says the LORD, who has compassion on you.

PHILIPPIANS 4:19

And my God will meet all your needs according to the riches of his glory in Christ Jesus.

LUKE 12:25–26

"Who of you by worrying can add a single hour to your life? Since you cannot do this very little thing, why do you worry about the rest?"

PSALM 56:3–4

When I am afraid, I put my trust in you. In God, whose word I praise — in God I trust and am not afraid. What can mere mortals do to me?

PSALM 9:9

The LORD is a refuge for the oppressed, a stronghold in times of trouble.

PSALM 23:4

Even though I walk through the darkest valley, I will fear no evil, for you are with me; your rod and your staff, they comfort me.

ISAIAH 41:10

"So do not fear, for I am with you; do not be dismayed, for I am your God. I will strengthen you and help you; I will uphold you with my righteous right hand."

LUKE 21:14–15

"But make up your mind not to worry beforehand how you will defend yourselves. For I will give you words and wisdom that none of your adversaries will be able to resist or contradict."

_____YOUR FAVORITE VERSES_____

Also available in the Daybreak series: